# ~Scribblings~

## From a Sidewalk Notebook

The Developing Life of Brad Brandon-Nead Sharp

by

Zaxxon Q Blaque

© *2009 by Brad Brandon-Nead Sharp. All rights reserved.*
*978-0-578-01636-8*

# Contents

Introduction ------------------------------------- Page 8

Poems ---------------------------------------------- Page 13

Songs ------------------------------------------------ Page 93

Quotes and Other Various Writings ------------ Page 121

Inspirational Others ------------------------------ Page 139

It Always Ends with a Little Something ------- Page 155

# Introduction

So, you're probably looking at this page and thinking, "Hmm, here's the boring part". Well, I'll agree with you on that one. Not only is this the boring part for me, I also find it the most difficult. When it comes to writing, I have emotions and a purpose behind it backing it up. This. This is something else entirely. I find it a little… void. The idea of just sitting and writing what my book and I are about without the motivations that I am accustomed to is unthinkable for me. To expect me to plop down random words to describe how I arrived at this point is a jaunting task which I will be very grateful to put behind me. Yet for you, as the reader, it's a necessity for me to summon the will and find the words for you so that you'll know what you've gotten yourself into. I started writing at the young age of fifteen. At the time I didn't really know what it was all about. The first poem I ever put into writing was meant to make a friend feel better about her self. She was going through some rough times and came to me for comfort. Through some kind of miracle, I was feeling what she was feeling. I was sympathizing, and I wanted to gather all of my abilities to make not just her feel whole again, but myself, too. This was my first taste of emotions, *real* pure human emotions. You are probably thinking that fifteen might be a little late in life to be experiencing this, and I'd agree with you, but my life was somewhat of an isolated one. I grew up away from the main part of town, away from interacting with my friends or any other people on a regular basis. In the years leading up to my emotional breakthrough, I had developed a world of my own self being to live and play in. Even though I was alone, I never felt it, but my world also kept others from getting through to me, which would prove to be self destructive later on in life. After spilling out onto paper what I was sympathizing for her, letting her glimpse into my being, and seeing the joy that derived from it, I was addicted. From the first few very simple and naïve scribbles that I used to understand myself and my constantly maturing emotional state, my writings evolved into a complex vessel for me to pour my raw conscious, and sometimes unconscious, being into, step back, and deal with them at my own pace. Sharing with other individuals and letting them see what I was going through and letting them know that they're not alone in the struggles of the everyday also proved to be a habit as well. I do believe that I have helped a lot of people just by letting them know I'm here and that I understand. Writing over the next few years, I have also helped myself cope with a variety of issues that are dealt with when growing up, especially since I never wanted to grow up in the first place. Isolation, sadness, rejection, death, joy, love, hate, anger, depression, suicide, sexuality, belonging, conforming, ignorance, tolerance, humor, comfort, beliefs, identity, and defiance are just a few of the subjects that are in this very tome. I noticed that as I grew, so did my writings. What started off as childlike simplicity became extremely complex and sometimes even hidden. I have included the date that each piece was written so I can reference what age I was going through each ordeal and how I chose to deal with it. This is as much a timeline of my story and evolution into adulthood as it is a collection of art or even possibly a guide for others. Yes, these are my views, my emotions, my method of coping in this very confused world, but I would be more than happy to share them with you. Who knows? Maybe I can reach more people than I ever thought I could and let them know that they are not alone and that there are people who care and who understand.

You are _never_ alone.

-Zaxxon Q Blaque

^_^

www.myspace.com/zaxxonq

# Poems

### To Friends I've Known 08-27-1995

The friendship we have is thicker than blood.
We've pulled each other out from the mud.
The bond we have will not let us part.
For the feelings we share all come from the heart.
The tie that binds us will not give way.
It will last eternally 'till our dying day.
So on this final note to our friendship that's long.
Divided we're weak but together we're strong.

### That Cold Touch of Death 08-28-1995

Why does he take the ones that we cherish?
The ones that we love and should never perish.
Feeling the numb hand fall on your shoulder.
As your skin turns white and your body grows colder.
When the curtain closes on the part you've played.
Now rest is the price you have been paid.
When you know you have lived in your final day,
and his silken flowing robe comes to embrace you away

### It 11-01-1995

It sits amongst prey, yet alone It will stand.
Lurking over the children, scythe shifting, hand to hand.
It is waiting...
It is choosing the one that It will take next,
to get rid of It's curse, It's horrible hex.
It is waiting...
It is tired of picking, so It selects them all.
Slicing them up and watching them fall.
It is taking...
With one mighty swipe, It takes the final one.
It is satisfied with what It has done.
It is aching...

### To the Friend I Knew 11-17-1995

"The friendship we have is thicker than blood..."

that's how the story went.

Now it seems to me that the friendship we <u>had</u>

was not heaven sent.

You carried away the friend that I knew

the one I loved and trusted.

Replaced her with something else that has

a heart terribly rusted.

I hate you, I despise you,

and directly to your face I say,

"I want my friend back, the one that I love,

the one that you took away."


### Ode to Life 11-20-1995

Darkness smothers, covers, and crowds me.

Have two eyes, yet cannot see.

You couldn't fathom the pain I feel.

To be rid of it, I would kill.

But to hide, I do lie.

Any more anguish and I shall die.

Suffered too long, Won't get along,

Today's society has gone so wrong.

My life is a bore, Can't take it anymore,

I'll jump from a cliff, so watch me soar.

My flight takes halt.

Yet it is no one's fault.

Now this is the end. So read it again.

Then close your eyes, and let the next problem begin...

### **No More** 11-21-1995

No more hunger.

No more pain.

No more suffering.

The world's insane.

No more sickness.

No more disease.

No more cancer.

God, help us, please!

No more hatred.

No more war.

There is no reason to

what we're dying for.

If we don't stop this,

I always knew:

there would be no more world,

and no more you...

## **Night of the Living Dead (a retelling)** 11-27-1995

Even while these words are spoken, the rising dead will take no token.

Killing people in their path, everyone will feel their wrath.

Taking ones that we love, with no help from up above.

They feed on flesh to survive. No more time to stay alive.

Finding shelter that will last, an antique farm house from the past.

She finds herself, soon, in distress. A newfound friend helps clear the mess.

From the cellar they heard a sound. Out of the door, new people bound.

Eye to eye, they do not meet, then madness starts like a slow beat.

By the thin threads they're hanging. Soon on the door dead will be banging.

Banging, breaking down the door, taking victims 'till no more.

Swiftly, heroine appears, facing all nightmarish fears.

Fighting 'till her final breath, giving them a second death.

Back to hell she regretfully sends, wishing for a happy end.

With mighty strength, help arrives, hearing all the dead's long cries.

Over heads they brutally beat, all while hanging them by their feet.

"They are us, and we are them", states Barbara's half delusional whim.

Torturing with such laughter.

Thus ends the story............... happily ever after?

### **The True Nightmare** 11-28-1995

Now I lay me down to sleep,
Tightly in my bed I curled,
With closed eyes I traveled deep,
deep into the slumber world.
Falling towards familiar ground,
Abruptly, I come to harsh, desolate land,
Behind, I heard the strangest sound,
It's the man with the razor hand.
With the claw dripping red,
We realize I'm the next life he'll take,
Grinning, he plunges at my head,
While I'm screaming, I awake.
Then I saw a blinding light,
With eyes widened, my heart stopped,
I grew cold, my hair turned white,
For I knew then the bomb had dropped.

**Monsters** 12-01-1995

There are monsters on this earth
who like to shoot and kill.
These monsters love to destroy,
and they'll do what they will.
They take no pity on the weak,
or those who "don't belong".
They do things to feel good,
even though they are wrong.
These monsters laugh when you're down,
they giggle when you're hurt.
They'll rub your face in the ground,
and make you eat the dirt.
Police have tried to stop them,
people have raised a fuss,
but there's nothing that we can do,
because those monsters are us...

## To Mothers Everywhere 12-04-1995

You have given me lots of things,
like love, hope, and joy,
yet I always ignored these things,
ever since I was a small boy.
I only wanted material things,
like toys, games, and money,
but as I look back through the years,
I find it kind of funny.
The things that kept me alive the most,
was you, your love, and care,
and I never gave a second thought,
of what a burden you must bear.
I will show you more respect,
no further will I bury the knife.
You've given me the ultimate gift,
and I say thank you for giving me life.

## The Silent Killer 02-04-1996

You've been a best friend most indeed,
you've managed to meet my greatest need.
To be a friend on which I can lean,
but lately you've been rather mean.
Your moods swinging left and right,
always looking to start a fight.
Crying 'till your eyes turn red,
wondering why you're not dead.
Bloating and pains while you pee,
and then blaming it all on me.
So take an aspirin and rest a while.
and don't let periods cramp your style.

### I'll Be There 02-25-1996

In desperate times my comfort you'd seek,
to wipe away your tear streaked cheek.
Your tormented heart I would tame,
and I know for me you'd do the same.
With my gift I'd make you smile,
then I'd make you laugh a while.
Temporarily your worries suppressed,
giving your broken heart a rest.
In return you would give to me,
a friendship lasting eternally.
I wanted suicide to take me away,
but you have given me a reason to stay.

### Rejection Junkie 06-27-1996

The locked away secrets were all to blame,
that stirred up emotions better kept dead.
Unstoppable feelings I couldn't tame.
By the hand, into darkness, I was led.
Flashbacks and memories of scenes long ago,
the wound in my gut has let them all spill.
With the truth out, I hung my head low,
frantically searching so the void I could fill.
The fire of my heart fed by faceless names,
has turned into an uncontrollable rage.
My tear stained pillow will extinguish the flames.
Not a chapter in my life, but just a page.
My shattered dreams lie on the floor,
hiding my head in shame and sorrow.
The awful sensations I had bore,
will arise and start again tomorrow.

### The Dawn Of Life (a little ditty) 05-01-1997

I have a friend named Dawn. She is a real cool chick.

She has a funny laugh.

That makes me really sorry I didn't know her sooner.

She has written some poems. That do not always rhyme.

I would go into detail.

But I do not have the present temporal measurement.

I really look up to her. I run when I hear her call.

The reason I look up to her.

Is because she's really vertically gifted.

This poem doesn't speak much of death, despair, or strife.

It's just here to remind:

we all have our Dawn of life.

### Forever Young (a bittersweet thought) 05-13-1997

We must toss away the old

to make way for the new.

"Don't look back", I've been told,

"to turn black skies into blue."

Blindly stumbling, forward marching,

taking friend's given advice.

"Forget what happened, it'll get better."

Covering heart-scars with bandages.

Head held high, but growing older,

living my life day by day.

I take a quick glance over my shoulder.

Now in the past I want to stay.

Loved ones jerk, tug, and pull me.

They force me to go on.

I remove the bandages from my heart.

Scars still present, everything better?

"Why can't we pick out the tid-bits of good times from the past and carry them with us into the future... forever?"

**Answers** 08-31-1997

Am I wrong in the things

I think?

Are my beliefs caving in

on me?

Is right really wrong; is wrong

really right?

Or is this all just pressure getting

to me?

Can I stay sane in an

insane world?

Will I make it; Just how strong

am I?

Why should I doubt myself and all

I know?

Or is doubt the next step toward

the truth?

### **Hidden** 09-14-1997

The voice inside me **hurts**.

Pondering to be or not **to**.

I am afraid for it to **be**.

Perhaps it should be **silenced**.

The demons in my soul **can**

quiet the rage that **I**

hid away to **save**

the demons from **myself**.

I only asked to **listen**,

for someone to talk **to**.

For nobody ever heard **their**

ancestors spin endless **stories**.

There was really nothing to cry **for**,

except the voice that's still **there**.

Sometimes I wonder if it **is**

searching for nonexistent **sanctuary**.

## **Treasure** 09-17-1997

Nothing in large quantities.

That's what this world has to offer;

nothing in large quantities,

and billions of people to spread it around.

People always say, "What if?"

"What if an opportunity could be taken, would you?"

"What if you kill in self defense, is it just?"

"What if there were other chances to find, would you look?"

Everyday, opportunities are given to you.

Anyone would take them, so would you, too.

If you must take a life to save a life, you may,

but you may not like the chances you find.

Naturally, I do not have all the answers.

If I did, I would gladly give them to you.

But don't fret, just be the human you are.

For those are the treasures in life we are all seeking.


"Quantities offer quantities around if you just look, you too may find answers you are seeking."

### **Walks Slowly Next To Me** 09-18-1997

In the glistening night, she walks,
taking off her silky skin slowly.
Shifting from one reality to the next.
Kissing the velvety dews of the lilies to
moisten her inner soul for me.

Her spirit caresses my heart as she floats by.

Gripping with gentleness to my stare,
I can't help myself, I must observe,
but shouldn't interfere with her nature
as she sings a song of ultimate beauty,
then sways to a song of bitter sadness.

I weep for her.

For she has been tainted and crushed
by the evil cruelties of the other world,
but here in the safety of my plane of existence
nothing can harm the purity of her soul
that I uncovered with laughter and understanding.

She softly weeps as I lovingly embrace her and stroke her radiant red hair.

### **The Crush (a companion to Rejection Junkie)** 01-17-1998

I thought it was all finally over

-my feelings suppressed-

After that last unfulfilling lover

-which left me depressed-

I thought the beast was finally dead

-run through the heart-

But yet again It raises It's head

-my overpowering counterpart-

Once again It stirs up those emotions

-the ones "better kept dead"-

It intoxicates me with It's potion

-"Live again", was all It said-

For awhile the feelings were nice

-to think there was another-

That could melt my heart of ice

-and take me a little further-

But I know this is all a game
-an elaborate tease-
Wildly trying to keep my heart tame
-so the madness doesn't seize-
To win this game is an impossible task
-for I'm the only player-
And the fabulous prize is beyond my grasp
-even with a mighty prayer-
But this time I will not weep
-I've played this game before-
My sanity and secret I will keep
-no matter how much I adore-
I've grasped the fact: "Won't land that dream boat."
-to dream the impossible dream-
Only my self made lies kept it afloat.
-it's easier than it seems-
It's left me a bit battered, beaten, and broken
-even a little flushed-
And through all this pain, I remember this token:
I now know why it's called a "crush"

### Lost Beginnings 01-18-1998

Can I retrace my footsteps, backwards,

through to my past?

No.

I find myself discovering present memories last.

All innocence discarded so easily,

like paper rubbish.

Play-time and laughter traded in, cruelly,

for heartache and anguish.

Was it my choice, though?

Could it have been stolen?

Yes, I think it was,

by an angel who had fallen.

Can I reclaim my

innocence lost?

Yes, I can,

but at too high of a cost.

I'd have to end my life,

where it is at present time.

Then start anew,

and savor each day in this child's lifetime.

But I'd be someone else,
I wouldn't be me!
And when I have to start again,
*then* who would I be?
That is too much to ask,
I'd prefer to stay here.
With the people I know,
the people who care.
And more importantly,
I would stay who I am.
As for things lost,
I couldn't give a damn.
If it's gone,
I won't chase or pursue.
I'll just cherish the fact there is a past,
although askew.
As long as I'm myself
with people who remember my past,
then it is not lost,
and I am found at last.

### Just Once (a prediction) 06-14-1998

Never a first time

and never again.

Never a second time

is always the case.

In this situation it's rare

that one would keep the words

with loved ones once shared

throughout the years.

Can't describe it, can't give it a face.

It's nameless in existence.

Fortunes once told crumble apart.

Falsifications sold at top dollar.

What is right, who is wrong?

Answers found dormant in the past.

Looking forward to a hopeful future.

Betrayed again by another.

Always a first time

and sometimes again.

Always a second time

is <u>never</u> the case.

"I wrote this piece out of the blue one day. At the time I didn't understand it. Later on that week, events unfolded to make me look back at this poem. I'll be damned if I wasn't trying to warn myself."

### **Schneider** 06-27-1998

There once was a pimp named Schneider.

Who had a girl and knew how to ride her.

When he learned she was rich,

He shot the poor bitch.

Then bought a brand new low rider.


### **Buzz** 06-27-1998

There once was a bro who was buzzin'.

For he drank his 40's by the dozen.

But now he's in A.A.

and sober everyday.

'Cause he learned he had slept with his cousin


### **Lessons Learned, Twice Taught** 08-05-1998

Beyond words. Beyond tears.

Beyond my fantasies. Beyond my fears.

Beyond silence. Beyond despair.

A pile of confusion, underneath, I am there.

I'm neutral to the world. My emotions gone numb.

How wonderful to be all blind, deaf, and dumb.

What a good actor I am! To show what is called for,

and keep everything else hidden, yet still know there is more.

The mistakes I've made were cause to emotional slips.

Letting only the truth flow from my lips.

I've observed my falls. Lessons learned, twice taught,

but to kill all my emotions is a battle still to be fought

**Publicity** 08-28-1998

Contours of beauty

Layers of pain

Lifetime of sacrifice

Such little gain

Hide the truth

Keep up appearance

Shield your face

Not given a chance

Is happiness achieved?

Dream of content

Joy tossed aside

For all it meant

The public eye

Sees only glam

As for suffering

Couldn't give a damn.

**Humanity** 09-03-1998

My name is not important.

People don't give a shit.

I can't alter their nature.

It's useless to throw a fit.

If I fail at the arcade

"YOU LOSE" flashes on the game.

Yet if I do the same in real life

the outcome will not be the same.

If I lose, I am a loser.

If I'm a loser, then I am lost.

If I am lost, I must be found.

I could be found, but at what cost?

Why does this world condemn the poor

to a lifetime of despair and sorrow?

I'll close my eyes, sigh, and die,

and look forward to a kinder tomorrow.

## The Dreamer Or The Dream? 01-19-1999

I wake up...

The world around me so foreign.

Is it real?

To find the dream within the dream, I drift in.

It's a nightmare!

Lively images of bitter dead ends.

Road to nowhere...

Yet up ahead, the road bends.

Which to choose?

One a game of fateful chance.

Should I choose!?

The other, a repetitive, mundane dance.

Am I ready?

Prepared to let go, on my own.

Confused by advice.

Yet the life I'm destined, they won't condone.

To be free!

Chasing dreams to bring ultimate joy.

Won't let go...

Held back by my roots as a boy.

I'm torn apart!

To know my destiny must be great.

Shatter my hopes...

Forced to follow my mother's fate.

My own identity.

Recognized for an awesome achievement.

Not given credit...

My only reward is to pay the rent.

Life supporting dreams.

Visions of my future keep me strong.

Goal blocking obstacles...

Will keep fighting, no matter for how long.

Suffocating, smothering love.

Hell, too much of *anything* is bad!

Need a push...

I know the truth will make us sad.

Let it go...

Learning as I leave the nest.

I'll be around.

With hopeful highs, I start my quest.

Always need you...

Your fond thought will lift my spirit.

Always love you...

I'll return, just keep the porch light lit.

I'll need support.

Can't go alone on my journey that's far.

The final act...

Will I be supporting character, or the star?

"Am I wrong for wanting a better, happier life for myself? Ah, to be a dreamer... what a sin!!!"

**Senses** 02-24-1999

To experience love-
You'll need all your senses.
Throw yourself in
abandoning all defenses.
To hear love-
Creeping up behind.
Ready to pounce,
and tease your mind.
To smell love-
Is an aromatic burst.
The more you inhale,
the more you thirst.
To see love-
Is a blinding vision.
Raw at first sight,
to proceed is your decision.
To feel love-
As a warm embrace.
A harsh emotional wave,
but as soft as lace.
To taste love-
Savoring such sour-sweet.
Will keep you grounded,
yet lift you off your feet.
To know love-
As the five senses entwine.
Takes a deeper understanding
and a handful of time.

**Too Much** 02-24-1999

Too shy...

-(silent words)-

Too afraid...

-(bottled feelings)-

Too alone...

-(better kept)-

Too long...

-(to myself)-

### The Right Of Passage 03-01-1999

To be a man you must conform.
To be a man armor adorn.
To be a man show strength so awesome.
Rejoice! Your right of pass has come!

To be woman you must obey.
To be woman throw dreams away.
To be woman play deaf and dumb.
Rejoice! Your right of pass has come!

To be a child no burdens you bear.
To be a child in simplicity you care.
To be a child, go on, have fun!
Rejoice! Your right of pass has come!

To be human is birth, suffering, and death.
To be human life in a single breath.
To be human today you're just a crumb.
Rejoice! Your right of pass has come!

Rejoice! You've learned to laugh at strife.
Rejoice! You've achieved compassion in life.
Rejoice! Silence is something you refuse.
Rejoice! With power you won't lose.
Rejoice! The complex test you've past.
Your right of passage has come at last!

**12-31-99** 03-03-1999

I had a dream of Christ reborn.
Wicked red with forked tongue and horns.
Promising utopia within brimstone and flame.
To heal the sickly, blind, and lame.
Telling stories of content and joy.
With evil smirk, he lays his ploy.
As soon as we follow anything he'll say,
slowly he takes his mask away.
Astounded, appalled, and shocked we stand.
Unveiled to see our creation of man.

**The Best Of Both Worlds** 03-03-1999

Pastures so green.
I long to be there...
A city so mean.
I long to be there...
Air so clean.
I long to be there...
Everyday a new crime scene!
I long to be there...
A happiness so pure.
I long to be there...
Hardships to endure.
I long to be there...
A loving embrace, so sweet to the taste.
I long to be there...
Heartbroken, rejected, my spirit infected.
I long to be there...
Surrounded by care.
I long to be there...
Alone in despair.
I long.....

**Forbidden Fantasies** 03-08-1999

A slap on the wrist,
a ticket to Hell,
in the end it's all the same,
now I pray my soul to sell.
To the highest bidder,
or a god that's not there.
The price to pay for lust
is too much for me to bear.
Wrestling and struggling with visions,
between possible love and pain,
throws me into the mouth of madness.
I find myself staggering, alone, in the rain.
I know I'll never find that "one",
who'll bring me happiness and damnation.
Guess I can cash in that ticket
as I stand proud in this fine nation!!!

**Religious?** 06-23-1999

Lords and Gods
All knowing, almighty!
Yet shed no tears for the tiny...
Lords and Gods
So brave, so tall!
Yet show no mercy to the small...
Lords and Gods
Creating life!
Then ignore their pain and strife...
In Lords and Gods
We place our faith.
You know their name, but not their face...

## Too Much Time On My Hands 06-25-1999

Envelope me in darkness

Embrace me in pain

Caress me with sadness

As I shun happiness in vain

Lovelorn and weary

Too tired to move on

Perhaps I'll stay here a while

To experience a bittersweet dawn

Cruel shadows scratching, lashing

Leave me in stitches

I don't mind the stings

Or the flesh that twitches.

Am I dead? Am I gone?

Or just perfectly lazy?

Time marches on and on

Yet my future seems hazy...

## My Friends 01-21-1999/06-25-1999

**D**arkness, **A** **W**riters **N**ectar

**M**yself, **I** **S**till **T**hrive **Y**outh

**S**adness **A**nd **R**age **A**ren't **H**ealthy

**K**arma **R**ises **I**n **S**ouls **T**hat **I**nspire **N**iceness

**C**an **H**appiness **R**eally **I**gnore **S**omeone **T**hat **I**s **N**ormally **A**lone?

**C**ould **Y**oung **N**aivety **D**ie **I**nside?

**D**eepest **E**bony **B**urrows **O**ver, **R**eady **A**nd **H**ellish

**H**ome's **O**wn **L**ove **L**ies **Y**onder

**T**oday **I**'ll **M**ourn

## A Lesson With Instincts (a story) 07-12-1999
### by: Brad Sharp & Misty Short

Let me tell you of a legend of a man, long ago,

conceived in the wilderness and born in the snow.

Fated to be a hunter, so bold, strong, & so brave.

He lusted for the kill, blood would be his only crave.

He was agile & swift & he traveled all the lands,

searching for prey which he would ravage with his hands.

In seasons of hard times, he could eat the meat raw.

Never waste a scrap, was his one and only law.

The man ran only on instincts, he was like an animal himself.

His only need was to survive, not worried about prosperity or wealth.

We can all learn a lesson about his story;

be brave, have courage and stay strong,

be true to yourself and you will never be wrong...

Don't look back on the path not taken

take the road you know is right.

To follow your heart, sometimes you must fight.

Do what you believe in, and always keep your goals in sight.

### **Good Mornin'** 08-15-1999

We tend to take things for granted:

The smell of a sunrise

The song of the trees

Conversations with a dog

The caress from a breeze

Dirt.....

Mother Nature to be specific

Wearing as little as possible

and to just know that it feels terrific.

Grass and weeds, but mostly weeds

Being in the moment

A hole dug by the dog

Not worrying for a word that rhymes with "moment"

Taking Father Time by the hand

and going for a little stroll

Just walking about the back yard

Watch out for that hole.

Smiling because you can

Followed by a little laughter

Taking a deeeeep sigh

Okay, a little more laughter

So if you like your coffee black

and a little part of you dies

As you fade into the darkness

remember to take a pocketful of sunrise.

### Lower The Torch, Lady 08-31-1999

When did we start to die?

Who gave us this wound?

Why did we provoke it?

Where is our tomb?

America, the beautiful!

Yeah, right!

America the crippled is more like it.

Will we ever see the light?

Promises, promises:

Fame, sex, wealth, love, shelter, clothing, food, a job.

Still waiting for pay day.

Now who does Mr. Hood rob?

Did I hit a nerve?

Probably not.

There's nothing under the flesh.

Just pure rot.

### Letting Go Of Tina 09-10-1999

You cry to me when you bleed,
yet if you prick me, do I not?
Tea & sympathy, a shoulder, and an ear.
The same from you was all I sought.
When I knocked, you didn't answer.
When I called, you were never there.
When I screamed, you covered your ears.
When I cried, you couldn't care.
You sapped away all I had.
Huh, I thought more highly of you!
I ignored everything others said to me.
I thought you'd stay as the girl I always knew.
I cannot wait for your next wound or whim
for you to come and see me again.
This game you play, I hoped you'd quit.
The truth is, you've driven me a little insane.
It's best to say good-bye now (as adults).
You can't look back, but remember this:
Don't ever forget the way we were,
for I'll always love you, Christina Davis

## (Living?) In The Real World 09-10-1999

My exposure to this world

has been brief, yet unique.

I've experienced many things.

A lot more than you think.

You can see the darkness,

the deepness in my eyes.

All the blame points to

this world's vicious lies.

What if I surrender to the black,

to the cold of the night?

It's a lot cheaper

than living in the light.

Let's look to the skies,

as our importance grows smaller,

and forcefully worship

the almighty dollar.

## My Heart Of Forgiving Nature 09-26-1999

Oh, my bleeding heart.

Come and bring your mop.

Sop up all that I've left you, and then wait for more.

Oh, my bleeding heart.

Stop squeezing me.

Not even a drop left. You've left me dry.

Oh, my bleeding heart.

I used to live, once upon a time.

Now, I'm a walking desert.

Oh, my bleeding heart.

Breathe new life into me.

It really doesn't matter, I couldn't care less.

Oh, my bleeding heart.

If there's no one out there,

I'll wait for the rain, and let nature take its' course.

## **My Dreams Are Mine** 10-07-1999

My dreams whisper to me-

I feel a breeze.

I shun it away.

Thought it a tease.

My dreams speak to me-

I hear a voice.

I must ignore it,

I have no choice.

My dreams scream to me-

A flash of lightning.

Hide my eyes and run.

Visions too frightening

My dreams abandon me-

I don't know my fate.

Now I know my dreams' plan,

and know it's also too late.

### **Me, Myself, & My Armor** 10-10-1999

Poetics - my mail.

To cushion the blows,

heart-ache, disasters,

and other life's lows.

Humor - my shield.

To fend off sadness,

depression, let-downs,

and debris left by others' madness.

Sarcasm - a sword.

To cut those down

before they get too close

and steal my crown.

My Armor - an excuse.

To deal with my doubt,

to stay happy,

and keep others out.

Inside the shell - a boy.

Quivering within, the real me

with exposed nerves and pure emotion

that no one can see.

Respect the Armor.

Respect the boy.

Respect the nerves.

Emotions aren't a toy.

"Living with myself isn't so bad..."

## Don The Masks (Each Other & Ourselves) 11-06-1999

We gain the wealth

Achieve the fame

To hell with health

To impress each other & ourselves

We don the masks

Dance at the ball

In faux glory light we bask

To impress each other & ourselves

Flutter a lash

Flaunt some ass

Light, inhale, flick the ash

To impress each other & ourselves

Cake on the face

Air out the wardrobe

Tonight, you're an ace

To lie to each other & ourselves

One night of fun

Don't get attached

'Cause it's over & done

To screw each other & ourselves

## **Solo** 11-11-1999

Isolation-

My elusive eternal dark lover,

my right hand man,

my security blanket under the covers.

Stare dumbfounded into the night.

A solo beat rhythms my heart.

Perspire steam and salt so sweet.

A single sigh just to start.

Exotic fantasies fulfilled.

Divine desires dreamt, live.

The darker the sin, the better.

Giving it all I can give.

Ecstasy discovered within thyself.

A good singer needs no band.

Who knows you better than you?

Practice makes perfectly talented hands.

## I 11-18-1999

He looks to the sky
with water in his eye
gives voice to a sigh
and starts to cry.
Was once told a lie,
was once told to die.
Just a normal shy guy
with a dream he could fly.
He thinks of days gone by-
An old ally,
his version of high,
the same question: "Why?"
Once believed he was sly
with his own alibi,
yet on this he can rely:
The end is nigh.

### **The Cold Front** 11-23-1999

There's a cold front movin' in-

Dark and brazen.

Swift like the night

and perpetually frozen.

There's a cold front movin' in-

Harsh and old.

Hidden away for ages

in the tales once told.

There's a cold front movin' in-

Take care to not get lost.

It has the pow'r to inhale steam

and exhale pure frost.

There's a cold front movin' in-

When you see it, flee.

You'll be sure to recognize it, though,

'cause that cold front is me.

## The Best Of Both Worlds 2 01-08-2000

I say, "Good night",

to sweet darkness-

Wrapped in black satin,

encased in the deep void.

I say, " Good mornin' ",

to the sunshine-

The happy content.

Conformation in joy.

I say, "Leave me alone",

to no one-

Mediocre aspirations

in a warm rut.

I see the dream-

The best of both worlds.

Yin and yang

thriving off each other.

### **You To Me** 01-11-2000

Radiant as the sun in the summer morn.
White and glistening as a unicorn's horn.
Uplifting, joyful, and fills me with glee.
That's what your smile is to me.
Sparkling beacons in the night.
Bright as light; an astonishing sight!
Gentle glances guiding; I see!
That's what your eyes are to me.
The best music I could ever hear.
Like ocean waves, so pleasing to the ear.
Little slices of heaven that set me free.
That's what your laughter is to me.
Advice given straight from the heart.
Morals in stories woven in pieces of art.
World's secrets locked away; you give the key.
That's your wisdom and love to me.

### **A Random Nothing** 02-23-2000

Words escape me and bounce off my ears.
Voided fantasies detect my greatest fears.
They roll down my head like darkened tears.
To think this is the best times in all my years.
I watch, in silence, the turning of the gears.
Laughing and pointing; these are my peers.
I shout out warnings, yet no one hears.
I admit defeat and toast them with cheers.

### **Where Are My Tears?** 03-06-2000

Joy makes a sorry inspiration.

That's why I long for cold.

My best works in art come from:

the dark, the black, the voided, the bold.

That's why this piece really sucks!

That's why it's over so fast.

I never thought I'd say this, but I'm finally happy at last.

Freedom....

### **Last Rights: An Epilogue** 03-10-2000

Say your prayers for you are mine.

Upon your supple neck, I dine.

Now taste of my forbidden wine.

Our loveless link boundless of time.

Let us bathe in crimson red.

Let me loose inside your head.

Listen closely to what is said.

Before you know it, you'll be dead.

Charmingly trance'd inside my spell

Bidding of all the tasks I tell.

Your victims blood, so sour to smell.

You'll wish you died and gone to Hell.

When you feel that we must part,

fashion a wood stake for my heart

Remember: always finish what you start.

Go, make me proud, my work of art.

### **To Whom...** 04-09-2000

To whom it may concern,

My life is but a tragedy.

To run, to flee, was my destiny.

Searching for joy within content.

Scrambling for ways to pay the rent.

Chasing those dreams without end.

Starting my own fashion trend.

Making new friends along the way.

Simply savoring each and every day.

Living my life to the fullest...

...what's the tragic part?

Is it possible for a person to live...

...without their heart?

What good is a heart if it's not exercised?

Sincerely, B.N.S.

### **Snowflake** 04-10-2000

He is born emerging from the clouds.

Fluttering softly, without a sound.

Amazed at the surroundings of the new world.

Gracefully falling, twirling around.

It seems like forever before he sees the ground.

Even then it looks like eternity.

Before his air-born adventure is over,

he wants to have fun while he's free.

First he does a dozen somersaults.

Then he does a trillion flips.

In his decent, he grows tired.

Everything aches, even his tips.

As he grows old, the ground grows close.

He looks back on his brief day.

Regretting nothing, he accepts his fate,

and finds a spot to quietly lay.

## **The Written Word** 05-17-2000

A wondrous thing, the written word:

It can build a kingdom,

or destroy and devastate a world.

Can nurture a growing relationship,

or crush the seeds of love.

Can be the cure for disease,

or the cause.

Can educate the sponge like minds of children,

if given the correct information.

If used wrong with falsities,

it can create a brain-dead future.

Can make you laugh; can make you cry;

Scream in terror; sigh in relief.

Can please an attentive audience,

or astonish and appall the elite.

Can make a statement with a sharp single sentence,

or baffle and confuse with vague chapters.

If used for truth, can bring down nations and civilizations.

If used for lies, brings wealth and fame.

One thing I've never seen the written word do

is lie to the writer.

### Just 20 06-23-2000

I've always wanted responsibility.

I forced myself to grow up.

Others encouraged this growth.

Now I find it's not enough.

I'm wide awake now.

I wipe the sleep from my mind's eye.

And now I see.

My life's just begun, and I cry.

The boy that died long ago

is resurrected from the past.

Given a second chance to live,

yet this time, not so fast.

I'm wide awake now.

I blink blur from my mind's eye.

And now I see.

My life's just begun, and I sigh.

I see my life.

I grab the knife.

I see my life

and cut the strife.

It's time for me

to be free.

Time for me.

Let me be.

Time for fun.

Life's just begun.

Games and fun.

My time in the sun.

I'm wide awake now.

Happy tears flow from my mind's eye.

And now I see.

My life's just begun, and I fly.

**Revenge** 06-30-2000

You watch me bleed, I watch you smile.
Sharpen the blade with a fine grain file.
You took my life, you took it all.
Used me to your whim, then watched me fall.
I never mattered. You fed your need.
I watched paralyzed. I still bleed.
So swift, so sudden, the attack but a blur.
Used my dream of love as your potent lure.
Hook, line, and sinker; I fell for the bait.
I tried to back out, but it was too late.
Another swipe at my heart. It's gone numb.
I see the evidence, now, and feel really dumb.
I took it in stride (along with half your stuff).
I made you disappear and made myself tough.
I've passed this test, I've walked the mile.
I watch you bleed. You watch me smile.

**Detour** 08-24-2000

Lost in the waiting.

Gave into confusion.

The ultimate desperation:

loneliness...

Reach for the nearest answer,

even the wrong one.

Of course, a mistake!

Left wandering, again...

A river ahead.

A murky flowing liquid.

I delve in the waters of lunacy.

I trip, and fall in...

Confusion, desperation, and pure madness

all sink in at once.

A dark haven comes to mind;

I dive in and say good-bye..

CPR, the breath of life.

A voice, "You have purpose, now live."

I get up, dust myself off

and continue my journey.

### **Rationalizing Suicide** 09-05-2000

My inspiration comes from pain.

My fame will come with my death.

I'm always late.

Might as well be early for *something*, right?

It's funny how the world works:

Those in need stay in need.

Those with wealth, gather more.

Children with toys who won't share.

I've cried too many tears (most held too long)

I've kept too many secrets (most not mine)

Felt too much pain (most self-inflicted)

Witnessed greed at maximum (most of it mine)

I want to sleep.

I want to hit the reset button.

I want to start again,

or at least stop.

Let me go.

There's nothing for me here.

Just people thinking of themselves.

Where's my ticket?

I'm too loved

I'm sorry for the hurt I caused (most accidental)

I'm sorry for the burden of me.

I give up.

### **Someday, Or At Least** 09-18-2000

Someday I'll be rich.

Someday I'll live in a mansion.

Someday I'll be somebody, or at least not a nobody.

Someday I'll make it.

Someday I'll find happiness.

Someday I'll sleep fine, or at least without pills.

Someday I won't know tears.

Someday I'll see my mom laugh.

Someday I'll fly away, or at least drive.

Someday I'll watch a movie without interruption.

Someday my phone will be mine, all mine.

Someday I'll sleep whenever and as long as I like.

Someday I'll be rich or at least not poor.


### **In Idle Imagery Nestling** 10-18-2000

I want to go home, but I'm already there.

I want to see them, but I don't think they care.

I've lost too many friends in all my years.

Now I want to find them and stop the tears.

I accidentally cut the thread to my past.

I want to mend it, but it's retreating too fast.

I'm afraid I'll lose them, along with my mind.

Never again will I find friends of their kind.

I now sit here waiting, wondering what's next.

I now sit here waiting and writing this text.

I'll sleep for now, but when I awake...

Now starts my search for my soul's sake.

### **Silent Offerings** 03-20-2001

I gave you a look.  You took it in silence.

I shivered and shook

at the first glance I took.

I gave you a kiss.  You took it in silence.

I cannot dismiss

that this is pure bliss.

I gave you my trust.  You took it in silence.

Celebrated in lust,

yet more is a must.

I gave you my love.  You took it in silence.

I prayed to above

that it would fit like a glove.

I gave you my heart.  You took it in silence.

That was the start

when we began to part.

You told me the silence was secrets,

and my gifts to you were nothing.

You had found another lover,

and put an end to our fling.

I gave you everything I had (all of me).

You crushed them to bits and returned them to me.

The jigsaw puzzle of my life

to assemble, once again, will not be easy.

**Destruction** 03-20-2001

You've broken my heart.
You've broken my spirit.
You've broken my trust.
Now you're going to hear it.
You've shattered my dreams.
You've shattered my hope.
You've shattered my love.
I don't know how I'll cope.
I believed your lies.
You believed mine, too:
you weren't really *that* good in bed,
but the love I felt was true.
You've destroyed my happiness.
You've devastated my life.
It will take time to move on,
but I will not grab the knife.

### **You're Real** 06-27-2001

I feel your touch, I taste your lips,
I smell your scent, I hear your voice,
I see your face, I know you're there.
I try to hold back, but I have no choice.
Your warmth surrounds me.
Your words cradle me.
Your presence comforts me.
Your caring fills me.
I hold you in my arms with disbelief.
You whisper to me a sweet nothing.
Slowly I open up my eyes...
You've vanished and left me longing.
I awake, violently, with a start.
You're next to me softly breathing.
I release a heavy sigh.
That's when I start believing.

### **The Scenes I've Seen** 11-06-2001

The scenes I've seen:

The human conflict-

The utterly tragic. The mentally scattered.

The impatiently troubled. The misguided rude.

The upset mother in a permanent mood.

The spiritually voided.

The blank pages filled with hate.

The lonely misery, just looking for a friend.

A smiling face, a cheery disposition,

a kind word, a silver lining to their grey day.

When faced with the negative,

just try your best

to cancel it out with the positive.

Don't do it for them,

but for your own peace of mind.

**When** 11-17-2001

When will I see it?
Misfortune's end.
When will I know it?
Eternity to spend.
When will I touch it?
A suffering bliss.
When will I taste it?
A sour-sweet kiss.
When can I believe it?
A mistold truth.
When can I live it?
A second chance youth.
When can I hold it?
A dream so dear.
When can I let go of it?
Burdens, doubts, and fear.
When can I treasure it?
A lifetime to spend.
When can I finish it?
The bitter end.

### **Infinity** 12-13-2001

My worries, my fears

my doubts, my years

in torture, in silence

in isolation, in science

I trusted, I turned to

I sacrificed, I still do

weep for them, weep for me

weep 'cause I can, weep for anybody

who'll listen, who'll understand

who'll sympathize, who'll lend a hand

to a nobody, to a fool

to the kind, to the cruel

a message to them, a message to you

an infinity loop, with no end to

my worries, my fears

my doubts, my years...

### **Beautiful Youth** 01-24-2002

Innocence cradles, naivety disables

doubt, worry, anguish, the scary

The youth so handsome, cumbersome

To potentially undo the world's view askew

Power in awe, shackled by modern law

The dances and songs, joy lasting long.

Immune to the virus created by us.

The cure in the doe eyes watching the skies.

Just watch, look deep, and that memory to keep.

Nourish your soul to fill that hole

Observe the child, pure and wild

Remember how you once were, holding the cure

Don't cry from memories, relive in stories

Beautiful youth again, with a hope it won't end

## **Davey Jones' Locker** 01-31-2002

Barbarisms in motion
Intricate human nature in flight
Consistencies in my mind
Structure I can not fight

She blames me for the world
Then turns and stumbles on her feet
I'm unaccustomed to this land
and this system I can't beat

A foreigner settling in
and everything expected of him
without knowledge, he will fail
Yet he tries on a whim

Smooth sailing from the start
The angry waters lie ahead
Confusion, stress, and damaging blows
lead to a life full of dread.

I want to jump and abandon ship
but I'm the captain and I'm going down
There must be a way for me to escape
and swim to shore before I drown

## Two Hands 02-17-2003

Two hands in light  
They feel the world  
Newborn delight  
In fingers curled  

Two hands at play  
They feel to learn  
Lessons everyday  
The soft and burn  

Two hands at work  
They feel the pain  
Hardships lurk  
Then comes the rain  

Two hands at rest  
They feel the weight  
Life's test  
The final fate  

Two hands pass on  
The world it tints  
Maybe gone  
Yet live in handprints

**A Life Like Mine** 04-06-2003

I want to rise above the world I'm in
yet I am afraid that I'm too deep under
So I sink further into the distortion
and I want to tear myself asunder

I play the part that I've been given
and secretly wish for a better role
I rehearse, practice, and fight
I'd even be willing to lose my soul

I see a place well hidden inside
A dark, cold, unnatural void
I curl up and nuzzle the lies
Now everything I've known is almost destroyed

Should I try again with the vengeful black?
Keep that dream and struggle uphill?
Or try to repair the life that I had?
Trouble is, I'm not sure what I still feel

I feel so numb and hollow
but still spark with the empty
I need to rise above
and take some time for me

Away from the madness and confusion
I hope to find some peace of mind
Still longing for and end to all
Who know what I will find?

### **Pondering** 12-01-2003

I don't want to become that statistic
A nervous bundle of consequence
A staggering story of failure
An end to justify the means

I don't want to fall into that category
The sorry excuses
The downtrodden resentment
The means to the end

Is it really so condemnable
to scan to the credits?
Hush hush, don't talk about it
It's better left sleeping

The ends and means
the categories and statistics
the stories, excuses, resentment, and failure
the ponderings of a human

**Worth It** 12-16-2003

Staring at the sun hurts my eyes

but the gleam, the shine, is so attractive

to touch it would be to totally combust

but it would be worth it.


Free falling makes me queasy

but the rush of adrenaline is such a high

to land would be disastrous

but it would be worth it.


Dying makes me cringe

but the hope of the end and answers allures

to expire would be definitive

but it would be worth it.


To love you is scary as hell

but the promise of a future beckons

to trust you is a risk

but it's worth it.

## I Know That You Love Me 11-19-2004

The effervescence & contagion of your personality
Warms me, makes me smile with comfort
Even though you cannot speak my language
You say thousands upon thousands of volumes
And I know that you love me

If I look into your green eyes & beg attention
I know you comprehend, nod, & deliver in confirmation
If I look into your blue eyes & beg for your kisses
I know you feel my need and you don't hesitate
And I know that you love me

I care for you & protect you
But that's only a small portion of adoration
You just have to look at me with head cocked
And I melt, and I'm yours
And I know that you love me

As we play, and pass the time
As we sit & stare, and as we nap
I know that you love me
And I love you too, my beautiful daughters

**Contradictions** 08-15-2005

Filling pages with thought
Filling minds with doubt
Giving voice to questioning logic
Giving logic the upper hand
Common sense is underrated
Common sense is endangered
Fighting against contradictions
Fighting contradicting believers
Believing history is learning
Believing learning is history
Knowing people will always hate
Knowing people will never change
Having love is a wonderful gift
Having love is a terrible curse

## Blue Collar American Zombies 08-15-2005

To be perpetually downtrodden,

a slave to necessities,

and not be given a chance to live in happiness and peace.

To be constantly worn-out,

spending every waking moment someplace else,

mustering the will to make a buck.

To be always asleep,

ever dreaming in the residence you're slowly killing yourself to keep

and use to store your ignored hopes that you never see with the open eye.

To be repeatedly lied to,

about becoming anything you want, about the freedom on layaway,

and that all people are created equal.

To be forever cursed,

with the burden to perceive the world and people as they truly are,

and never have dry eyes.

To be permanently stressed,

on edge, ready to jump,

yearning for the quiet comfort,

but hey, you have love and running water.

**Always…** 08-17-2005

Always late
Always tired
Always broke
Always stressed
Always hungry
Always bored
Always sweating
Always depressed
Always hopeless
Always restless
Always grumpy
Always dreaming
Always angry
Always teary
Always pushing
Always working
Always hot
Always crowded
Always walking
Always awake
Always uncomfortable
Always hurting
Always wanting more
Always getting less

**David** 01-08-2006

Care to imagine the taste of learned experience,

to drink deep, full of it's knowledge.

To bask in bathed light, kissed with hints of history,

caressing ignorance away.

Dare to be cut harsh by boundless blades of brutal mistakes

so hurting to never crave pain again.

To finally see self inflicted worrying wounds of widespread wars

and patch them up without peeking at the scars.

Bear your own cross to heal once and for all on your own

and know you've triumphed yourself through every obstacle.

Look back at razor eyes, the jealous slits,

absorbing all the suffering you have left behind.

Look ahead, move forward,

and take that first fleeting step towards freedom from loss.

Will you ever open your eyes, tear them up, or awaken silently to know this to be true to every punctuation

and trust the help that's thrust so desperately at your feet?

### **And The Light Shined Upon This Boy** 05-23-2006

And he felt the warmth, he saw the glow
Only good things is all he'll know
And the boy grew up bathed in light
Yet, he saw the shadow, and not so bright
And he wandered far from his home of shine
He wanted the darkness, "I'll make it mine"
And he nestled deep within the dark
He held it close and bared the mark
And the empty void grew so cold
It hurt him, teased him, and bled him ten fold
And the boy wondered why he left his kin
To forge a deal with the angry and sin
And he wrestled hard with the soulless black
He wanted the love and the sunlight back
But his dwelling resides now bleak within
Will this boy ever find his way back, again

### **Then...** 05-25-2006

Then all the wicked went away
We'll dance and sing and praise and play
Have the moment, until the day
The wicked come back to rest and stay

### I Hope He's Worth It 05-25-2006

I hope he's worth the pain I have
The tears I've cried
The sleepless nights
Endless thoughts of him
Of us
Of what we've shared
Our connection, our bond
That which was broken
A sacred trust foolishly given
I also hope he's worth what he has caused
With his decision
His ultimate choice
Right or wrong
He chose to hurt
I only hope
He doesn't do
What he did to me
What he'll do to you

### Would Anybody Want? 05-25-2006

Would anybody want a man who's loyal

Loves with his all, despite the turmoil

Would anybody want a man with emotion

To laugh, to cry, have sympathy and devotion

Would anybody want a man with more

Not just a pretty face, but a solid inner core

Would anybody want a man who looks beyond

The physical, the body, yet sees it just as fond

Would anybody want a man who had love

To know it, to recognize it when sent from above

Would anybody want a man who's a bust

At life, at relationships, and earning other's trust

Would anybody want a man who's been hurt

By loss, heartache, and a straying flirt

Would anybody want a man so true

That man is me, now where are you?

**Prototype** 05-29-2006

On the assembly line, I had a flaw

To have a heart so pure and raw

My makers tried to keep me sheltered

Only to make progression haltered

I knew nothing of the definition of pain

How to handle, and deal, with all life's disdain

Version 1.0 was the quivering boy

So scared of the hurt, despite all the joy

I was then remodeled with plates of forged steel

To defend the bruised heart, to help it heal

A stronger version, 1.1

Retooled to react to pain and run

Longing for love, I sought out a goal

To find the other half of my tortured soul

I tooled and I tried to break down the walls

Version 1.2 had its many stalls

Still too cautious of the grandeur of life

Paralyzed from the past with misery run rife

I lubricate my gears and forward I grind

Hoping for that love that I would soon find

Not afraid, but naïve was 1.3
Finding love everywhere, but still too blind to see
Version 1.4 had to finally wise up
I learned about sacrifice, arguing, and to makeup
Relationships were formed, a lesson to learn
I'd soon find out how that love could burn
Re-mastered and remade to 1.5
Then soon found a switch simply marked "override"
The barriers now down, I let myself go
Never suspicious of that hard first blow
System failure, I'm back to 1.0
Devastated by the single word "No"
I pick up my pieces, my blueprint, and plan
To build myself up to be the better man
I am not perfect, not do I claim to be
I am just a prototype to the final version of me

### **For Scott** 06-02-2006

The pain you have that I once had
Never to know the touch of love
There was a glimpse that soon turned bad
Too late to know the true meaning of

I see your tears dwell deep inside
You saw my tears fall from my face
Your demand of time I must abide
Just know you never fell from my grace

I know we had something special with us
I know there were mistakes on both ends
I know that we have a lot to discuss
I know that I don't want to stop being friends

What the future will hold, we may never know
We will pull though this huge disaster
Always close to my heart you'll flow
You're on my mind, Scott Hugh MacMaster.

## My Perfect Companion 08-16-2006

My eyes squint to shut out the dull sting given by gazing upon your intense shine and ample brilliance never-ending.

I'm attracted to your radiance so bright, like a moth to a flame, yet I know this time I will not be burnt.

As my pupils adjust to this new magnitude of light, I stare blank and dumb in amazement with a permanent expression of awe etched on my face.

I question if I am worthy of such a glorious treasure that offers me endearing emotions so true not yet tasted before but easily recognized on the palate.

Now knowing the hand of fate played a role, I open my heart, close on an embrace, and I know that I am truly loved and in love with my perfect companion.

More than words, my love…

## **Never Endeavor (Dreamer, Surrender)** 11-13-2007

Wasted are the years I've spent
Flowing deep with regret & sorrow
Still, I know not what it meant
To idle & wait for tomorrow

Inconstancies I abhor
Haunt my endless waking dreams
Fighting mundane leaves me sore
& stifles twilight limbo screams

Curling into quiet ruts
To me always equates death
Allowing wounds & fatal cuts
Caused by stillness of my breath

I flail forward futilely in place
Forward steps slide me further back
No matter how I change the pace
It's the means & drive that I lack

## **Hard** 01-15-2009

Choking on my own sobriety, I have nothing to say
Missing all of the solemn inconsistent intricacies
I swallow freedom hard and chase it with dollar bills
Hoping that would stifle the bitter taste that invaded my agape mouth

The laughter came as a surprise in the early morning light
It shook me awake, even more conscious of my own nature
I sigh hard with spittle flung on my arm
I smile knowing that it was the last

He muttered something that I didn't catch
Yet I understood all while hanging on his every word
I listened hard for the syllables that I had so longed for
Never realizing that they had been said already a thousand times over

Growing, nurturing, quiet, calm riot
Unaware, sentient, gentle forces
Swelling silent and raging hard
I still walk on, march forward, still here

### **Tangled & Twisted** 03-10-2009

Depression settles in, something hard to ignore
It hits you like a sledgehammer, knocking you to the floor
As you crawl to your knees and beg it away
You tremblingly realize it is here to stay

The struggle ensues that leaves you broken weak
A humble mundane mediation is all that you seek
No longer yearning bliss, just an end to the pains
But its roots set in deep, crawling beneath your veins

The branches stretch slyly out, consuming you complete
Your legs dangle madly in hopes of swift retreat
You try a primal scream, but are stifled by the limbs
A slave to its sway, steadfastness, stagger, and stark whims

Tears gush out fierce and roll slowly down the leaves
For a moment all is still as the oppression reprieves
Softly shrinking, withering, then finally buried
Paused in wonder why you planted that wicked seed

# Songs

**Shun** 04-08-2001

Searching for something to believe in
Someone that I knew was real
Though I try, I cannot find it
Now it seems that I can't feel
You took away the best of me
And left me with this shell
Now I've returned to reclaim myself
And send you straight to Hell

I never wanted it to end this way
I just wanted you to go away

I'll shun you away, I'll shun you away
Don't look my way, I'll shun you away
Won't lead you astray, just shun you... away

I've learned a lesson in this game
I won't treat you like you did to me
It's time to move on from here
Fly from your grasp and be free

I didn't want to feel this way
I just wanted to go away

I'll shun you away, I'll shun you away
I'll leave you at bay, and shun you away
Face my new day, I've shunned you...

The gentle looks you gave to me
Your soft voice saying you won't leave
You locked the door and stole the key
I shall not wait, I will not grieve
The pictures that you painted me
Are all now just a memory
There's nothing left for me to say
So I'll just simply shun you away

In your arms I wanted to stay
Now I know that you don't feel that way

I'll shun you away, I'll shun you away
The price you will pay, I'll shun you away
The games that you played, I've shunned them away
Dark clouds turn to grey, I'll shun them away
A brighter new day, I've shunned you away.

**Dreamer** 04-11-2001

Dream on, Dreamer, dream on (x4)

Look out
I might think of you
Recall the way we were
and then start feeling blue
Look out
Don't you see me there?
Standing in the shadows
Don't you see, or don't you care?

I used to think the tide would change
I used to dream my life away
I used to think that we could be
Now I have to face reality

Dream on
Dream on, Dreamer, dream on
Dreamer
Don't wake the Dreamer or the dream will be gone

You
Don't you think of us?
Remember days we spent
in wild actions of our lust
You
Don't you ever dream?!
To shape your fantasies
to a happiness that you deem
I used to think that you could care
I used to think you would play fair
Now I see how you treat me
This is the harsh reality

Dream on
Dream on, Dreamer, dream on
Dreamer
Don't wake the Dreamer or the dream will be gone

The time it took
For me to see you are not real
and choke down that bitter pill
Close the book
On that chapter of your lies
and cut the bind of those tainted ties

Dream on
Dream on, Dreamer, dream on
Dreamer
Don't wake the Dreamer or the dream will be gone

You've awaken me...

**Losing It** 04-26-2001

More than once I've seen some things
that were not there, I've heard some things
come from somewhere that could not be
except from deep inside of me.

You've come along
You say you want me, though I can't believe it.
Are you for real?
I try to answer but I've gone silent.

You approach me, but I wouldn't recommend it.
I close my eyes and shake my head
'cause I think I'm losing it.

I've gone crazy, lost in madness
I've been insane, trapped in sadness
I know my brain has dreamt some things
I can't believe, now my soul sings

You hold me
You say you're there, but are you a figment?
Someone pinch me
Wake me up before I start to feel it

You approach me, but I wouldn't recommend it.
I close my eyes and shake my head
'cause I think I'm losing it.

You see it now from my point of view
An end to my insanity is way past due
I see you now, you're heaven sent
but I still say that I'm losing it

You're everything- I could ever want and then some
I never thought- Someone like you would ever come
I can believe- In my love, and I'm gonna use it
Everything is fine- I guess I was just losing it.

**Living In My Dreams** 05-23-2001

I close my eyes
As I drift I feel at peace
I'm going home
I belong here and not that other place
I'm searching
For something that can't be found
I'm alone
But at least I'm safe and sound

You look but you never do see
I'm crying down on my knees
I'm only living in my dreams
Never have I tried to escape
'Cause I know it's much too late
I'm only living in my dreams

I miss the risk of bliss in this kiss
I know the seeds I sew will grow from down below
I feel the deal is real to fulfill the meal from the first kill
I'll wake and break the fake and make the take for my own sake

That search that will never end
To take whatever you send
Is only living in my dreams
'Cause I know in the back of my mind
That love that I never will find
Is only living in my dreams
Only living in my dreams

**Direct Me** 06-12-2001

Black satin, velvet ropes
Flashing lights and high hung hopes
Designer labels and French cologne
All to cover up the fear of being alone

Sleazy agents with spray-on tans
Autographs for screaming fans
Hollywood: the glitz and fame
Popularity: as fickle as a flame

You tell me
How to look, how to act,
sign a deal that feels like it's real
Tell me; How to dress, how to play this game,
what not to say, yet I say it anyway.

I'm gonna do what I want
I'm gonna feel how I please
I'm gonna go where I wanna go
No one's gonna direct me

You cut my ties to my family,
and my friends can only see me on the T.V.
I was happy 'till I was found
Now I want a way down to touch ground

Because you tell me

When to smile, when to cry,

when to scream and show the anger in my eyes

Tell me; When to sleep, when to wake,

when to fake the face for the last take

I'm gonna do what I want

I'm gonna feel how I please

I'm gonna go where I wanna go

No one's gonna direct me

Bleach the teeth, dye the hair, change myself again

Don't get fat, start the diet and fitness plan

Represent as the perfect model spokesman

When will I ever feel like myself again?

You tell me, tell me

You tell me.....

It's my name on the line

You will no longer confine

Time to settle the score

and I'm not gonna take this shit anymore!

I'm gonna do what I want

I'm gonna feel how I please

I'm gonna go wherever the hell I wanna go

No one's gonna direct me

**Prisoner of My Mind** 08-14-2001

He wants to live the silent dream
The vivid life that it must seem
Traces of the human kind

He wants to live before he dies
Yet on the ground is where he lies
Escape the void inside the mind

He wants to laugh, but for now he'll cry
One day he'll sing, one day he'll fly

After the pain I expect the joy
End the torment and free the boy
Inside
My mind
Prisoner of my mind

He sees the goal is close at hand
But as he walks so shifts the sand
Oasis built by the blind

Even as the sun beats down
He will not sleep, he will not drown
Treasure all that you find

The obstacle or a mindless task
He'll overcome all and in glory he'll bask

After the pain I expect the joy
End the torment and free the boy
Inside
My mind
Prisoner of my mind

And somewhere sometimes this boy will sigh
Look to the sky with stars in his eye
He was told he would never get that high
Now I'm left here to wonder why...

They'll watch and wait for him to fall
But he'll show the world, he'll show them all

After the pain I expect the joy
End the torment and free the boy
Inside
My mind
Prisoner of my mind

### I Wanna Go Out with My Baby 01-18-2003

I wanna go out with my baby
I wanna go out and see
I wanna go out with my baby
and see if baby is in love with me

I used to think that circumstance had a hand
in our meeting
But now I know how our love grows
it's because fate started our heart's beating.

I wanna go out with my baby
I wanna go out and be free
I wanna go out with my baby
and see baby in love with me

Can this be happening to me?
I've been given a second chance.

To love and live
and take and give
and share a heart and my hand
I've thought of all
and found my call
to stand beside my man.

So, I wanna out with my baby
I wanna go out and just be
I wanna go out with my baby
'Cause my baby's in love with me.

**Totally Loving You** 05-23-2004
*(Previously unfinished – finished 03-10-2009)*

Stop me if you've heard this tale
Of a love over e-mail
What started small became so huge
But I'm sure this is old news

Y'see, this broken boy was taken
And his tired heart was aching
For someone new

He options for a night of fun
Maybe just hang out with someone
He jumps online to find a friend
And finds his search comes to a quick end

Now the lights don't seem so dim
Since he found someone like him
Out of the blue

At first it isn't what we meant
It was all just a crazy accident

I am totally - Loving you loving me
Broken hearts heard fate call
That made us meet and made me fall

Then the tale takes a turn
The staleness makes us twist and burn
We fight that fire with our flame
But in the end we're both to blame

We let that love slip away
Now this is the price we pay
For our mistakes

We struggle hard day and night
Anything to start a fight
Through it all we're both still there
The love's still strong, we both still care

Set aside our separate view
We are willing to do
Whatever it takes

At first I thought that it was fate
But now I know that you're my soul mate.

I am totally - Loving you loving me
I'll be your strength when weakness crawls
You'll be my light when darkness falls

No relationship is perfect
But I know that we can work it through
It's more that I could predict
But everything I do, that I say, that give, that I take, that I fix, that I break,
that I fight, and then surrender myself all to you, all for you

I am totally - Loving you loving me
Broken hearts heard fate call
That made us meet and made me fall

I am totally - Loving you loving me
I'll be your strength when weakness crawls
You'll be my light when darkness falls

## **Why Bother?** 11-01-2004

Who needs the stars?

When you've got all these pretty lights?

Under a darkened, cloudy, hazy sky

Why bother now?

Who needs the dirt?

When you've got sturdy cement?

Intersecting highways and pavement

Why bother now?

The earth is lost and so am I

Why should we care, why should we try?

Technology is the future now

Listen to me, I'll tell you how

Who needs the woods?

When we've got a thriving city?

Tall skyscrapers and looming buildings

Why bother now?

Who needs the sun?

When we've got electricity?

Nuclear power and efficiency

Why bother now?

I thought I heard Mother Nature cry
Pass her a tissue, don't ask her why
We must focus on prosperity
What the future holds, just wait and see

Who needs the stars
When you've got all these pretty lights
Under a dying, toxic, lazy sky
Why bother?

## The Fairy Tale Ends 01-09-2005

There's a sickness that afflicts us
All
In America
No solution to a problem
Caused
By Americans

One nation under God, the invisible man
He disappeared with our highest hopes
Where was he when we needed Him the most?
He was gone…
…and the fairy tale ends

There's no happy ending, no Prince Charming
Just a
"Once upon a time"
The story was told, we believed those lies
That was
Our greatest crime

So don't tell me to take the blame and run
I'm not the only one at fault
You still look to the skies like you did back then
But it's wrong…
…and the fairy tale ends
…and the fairy tale ends

They lie to you, they lie to me
Lives pile on the ground, why don't you see?
Truth stares you in the face, you look it right through
Embrace the warm lie you've grown used to

Then when it all goes wrong
Like so many times before
You pin the blame on others
To even the score

Retaliations run high with no reason for

but the story told before

It's all wrong

and it's all gone…
…and the fairy tale ends

## I Surrender (On My Knees) 07-25-2005

Never have I ever needed to have
Never have I ever needed to hold you
Never have I ever needed you so bad
Never have I ever needed, but I do

This is not how I thought that it would go
Cross that line, take my time, nice and slow
This is not how I thought that it would be
So intense, my defense has abandoned me

You love like you're fighting a war
I surrender, I can take no more
Do with me as you please
As I fall on my knees

Never have I ever waved the white flag
Never thought that I would be the one to
I only saw love as a burden to drag
Then you came along and made that untrue

I'm disarmed by your charm, you're so special
Enraptured and captured by your flaming vessel
Take a part of my heart and of my soul
Tempered, burned, and returned to make me whole

You love like you're fighting a war
I surrender, I can take no more
Do with me as you please
As I fall on my knees

Desperately I look to you, hoping you would have a clue
Nestled in your eyes of blue. Tell me what I have to do.
If I fall, will you fall too? All the time I knew you knew
Tell me what I have to do. Tell me what I have to do.

You love like you're fighting a war
I surrender, I can take no more
Do with me as you please
As I fall on my knees

Do with me as you please
As I fall on my knees

# Quotes
# and Other Various Writings

## **Alone** 10-21-1997

The madness of isolation is tearing me apart from the inside, feasting on my innards to satisfy their hunger of relentless tormenting that shall prove to be eternal. My insanity is but a drop in the endless, horizon kissing, ocean of despair that has enveloped this cruel, unforgiving, power-hungry, planet. All the bits of light which offered happiness, laughter, understanding, and friendship have either shattered, faded, or has been crudely fused from other shards of long past which are still hued with the original dirt and darkness.

The outward actions of joy I've been performing are nothing more but an act to please others and shroud my true self of pity from them and myself. Poetics cannot shield me from the barricading, and eventually seizing, of the dementia that I have foolishly taken as a shelter. For the false asylum is tumbling, and I can no longer linger.

I must escape! Escape before I am crushed and overtaken by the mania. The madness in which I am strung up as some deranged puppet, a mere shell of myself, unknowing of the puppeteer's identity or plan for me. Doing his bidding with no will of my own, and all while donning a painted smile. The decision is clear. I must escape!

## **Scream** 01-23-1998

The languages I speak are either foreign to most or fall

upon deaf ears for no one seems to understand me.

All information is present on the page; there are no secrets

kept from anyone, yet it seems the facts elude the people I

want to contact the most.

Am I just babbling nonsensical text that only I can

translate for the narrowly confined clan which are my friends?

I need a way to reach the ones I care for who seem thousands

of miles away.

My messages in the bottles I send to drift towards them never

seem to get washed upon their sand smeared shores.

If only I could yell loud enough...

### **Meditate** 04-06-1998

Stop...

Breathe...

Take a second...

Just a second...

Smell the roses...

Now...

### **WAKE UP!!!**

Turn around to face yourself to see what you're doing.

Get a grip!

It's not the end of the world...

it's just the beginning!

Now... meditate...

### **Allergic To The Wants Of Others: an ode to customers** 05-11-1998

"I have money to blow, do you want it?"

"Just give me something I don't need and can't find."

"I know you're busy with three other people, but do you think you can squeeze me in?"

"Then, after you're through, I'll either forget something else or yell at you at the top of my lungs."

"Thanks for all your help. I'll be sure to come back and gripe some more."

"My goal in this isn't good service, just to get you fired and miserable."

"I'll be sure to recommend you to my friends!"

## A Skeptic 01-19-1999

Here I sit, alone and unsure, pondering the same questions over and over in my mind:

"Is it morally wrong to love another, despite their age, color, religion, and yes, even gender? If love is supposed to be the greatest thing ever in the world, then why are there limitations on who you can and cannot love? Why is it so "wrong" and socially unacceptable to be in love with someone who doesn't fit <u>others</u>' standards? Who the hell has the right to tell me who I can and cannot love?! If Hell is supposed to be for sinners, and love isn't a sin, yet if you happen to fall in love with someone of the same sex, then you're going to Hell, then aren't you just damned for loving and caring for another human being? Does this make sense?"

Answer these questions for me, (Mother), if you can.

"If I go to Hell for loving, then the whole world should be right on my heels. How can I believe in a god that would let this happen?"

## Talking To A Brick Wall 03-05-1999

I stare at a blank page
wondering what's hidden within.
I stare at my blank heart
wondering if there's anything left.
You've stolen all energy present
with spiteful tongue and hateful glances.
Contaminated something so pure.
On purpose, or accident?
You want me to join you
in self pity and isolation.
You drag me under...
Drowning me below currents so cold.
Why can't you cut the shackles that bind you?
Sever the chains to your past, your father.
Live a little, and relax. It won't hurt.
Enjoy a moment for the moment.
Open yourself to the innocence that once was,
or at least let me go
to live a happy life to the fullest.
You can watch me prosper.
Careful, you might crack a smile.
Why can't you live?
I hate to see you dying so slowly.
It pains me to see you fade.
Yet if that's what you want, so be it!
Just don't take me along for the ride.
I've already been there.
Why does it feel like I'm talking to a brick wall?

## Aqua 10-19-1999

As I breathe in the weight of the world a soft hue of blue enters my body and takes over. I am compelled to swim the ocean. My mind is lost to the sea, the unorganized, unforgiving waters that I now gasp for. Waves roll overhead as I sing with the whales their solemn song. I've lost all feeling in my head and heart. When I'm sure I'm tucked in as far as I'll go into the cobalt madness, such so that not even the best seafaring man could see me, I cry. I weep out all that was in me, releasing all emotions: the torment, the anger, the sadness, the torture, the rage, the despair, the loneliness, the utter feeling of hopelessness pour out, making the ocean deeper and a darker tint with every sob.

Still, no one hears me or pays mind to the ever rising tides.

No one...

I'll stop only when I feel I've done my part in placing as much of myself as I can into the waters. With the final gush, I'll wring myself out of all the heaviness of the darkened fluid, and rise towards the surface. I'll find myself floating weightlessly above the splashes that grasp in vain at me with every movement. I'll land back on my island and fill up once again...

## Eyes Open Wide 10-25-1999

So, where do I go from here?

I wait for someone to point me in

the right direction even though

I know that no one will show.

Being in the middle has always been

fine for me, but still I dream of

better and fear the worst. Perhaps

that's just the human in me.

At least I'm not waiting alone...

## Helpless 01-24-2000

You make me crazy, yet keep me sane.

I'm flying with both feet on the ground.

I could care less about you,

but I miss you with all my heart.

I don't know how to describe what I'm feeling,

but I've heard this song before.

I wanna cry; I wanna laugh;

I wanna kiss you; I wanna destroy you.

I want to drive you away, but keep

you close to me.

I want you all to myself,

but have to share you.

I'm angry with what we said;

I'm angry with what we did;

but I wouldn't change a moment of it.

I lose the words,

but when you're around, I find them.

You've been there my whole life,

yet were hidden in plain sight (I should've acted sooner).

Would it have made a difference if you knew what I was feeling   and thinking the whole time I knew you?

I've lost you already,

and I can't do a thing about it.

### <u>Triple Reject</u> 04-10-2000

She...

She sees me.

Sees me as an idol.

I...

I see him.

See him as a soul mate.

He...

He sees her.

Sees her as a piece.

They...

They see us.

See us as fucked up.

We...

We see them.

See them as ignorant.

### <u>Gratitude To 24 Hours</u> 07-26-2000

It's so utterly fascinating what difference one small day can make. Your life is headed one way, with some things and people standing to face you and all other people and things stand with their backs to you. Then "the" day comes along. Twenty-four anything-but-ordinary hours that swoop in and turn most things, if not everything, a complete 180. Hell, some things are turned upside-down as well as around! So odd. I've always taken time for granted and always wanted to rush things, but now I find myself enjoying everyday seconds. Savoring every drop of time in each day. Counting my breaths. Watching a caterpillar drip like molasses down a twig of leaves. Watching the full effect of bread cooking. Doing absolutely nothing, and loving it. All thanks to those days that turn our world topsy-turvy, back again, and then maybe turvy-topsy.

### **Quotes From The Mind Of Brad Brandon-Nead Sharp**

"We allow the madness we create...
and only we can turn our backs to it"

"It's true; nobody actually <u>needs</u> somebody,
but it sure is nice!"

"She says I wallow in self pity,
but is she trying to see herself in me?"

"Why should I wait on those who won't?"

"Chaos, mayhem, confusion!...
and that was just this morning's dishes!"

"Today didn't even exist yesterday!"

"A little pain never hurt anyone."

"Why are we born with innocence in a world
where it is just stolen later?
Was there a point to this plan,
'cause I must've missed it!"

"Everyday, I have to cry
to wet my eyes so I can see
and not miss any opportunities
of happiness that come to me."


"My love for you is like an apple on a branch:
If left alone, it will ripen,
but be wise of when to pluck it,
for if left too long, it will rot and fall
& a new love will take it's place"


"True love is like a four leaf clover
Very rare and hard to find
When I found I looked it over
I cursed my eyes for being blind"


"People always want ample amounts of sugar
to sweeten their life up,
Yet they should learn to take the bitter.
It's an acquired taste!"

## **The Never-ending... You Know** 01-30-2002

This is not the same story, yet it's been heard before

I've told it many times, but no one listens

The same story, a different version

The names changed to protect the innocent

A unique time, another place

Covered eyes, but ears wide open

So, here's the plot, modified to fit the screen and time allotted

Edited for life-like violence and fucking language

Pardon my Italian

Two lives, intertwined...

or was it a knot?

Fated to be bound and bound to be fated

A glance, a look...

Huh, what's the difference?

Does it matter?

Not anymore, but maybe a little to me.

Oh yeah, the story...

Waiting for the end?

Too bad, so sad, it doesn't

It's still playing at your local theater

My life

Could it be?

A case of mistaken identity?

Two babes switched back at birth?

Nah, not that lucky, but lucky enough

Found my dream house, my dream car, and even my dream guy,

none of them pink, by the way

Except sometimes my guy

Just waiting for my cue

Reach that point

Acquired that happy medium,

but still waiting for eternal bliss

So what next?

That's for all of us to see

The End...

...for now

### Rushed Salvation 02-05-2002

Can you help me?
I've seem to have lost my way
I'm not sure where I'm headed to
but I hope to arrive today

My stomach is empty, my mind is full
I carry the burdens of the world
I'll cry a river of my own tears
and set my sail to unfurl

### Lost Another Again 08-05-2002

She's gone from my life for good this time
There was nothing I could do
She just slipped away
As I held my own tears
The memories haunt me
Like a tease of times that will never be again
Although my heart breaks
And the familiar pain sets in
I won't let it take over
It's happened too many times before
And maybe again
So I just open my hand and let her go
To wander in the madness and isolation
I'll let her feel what it's like
I will not rescue her
Or wait her return

### The Animals 08-01-2004

I witnessed the worst of humans all in one day. It hit me like a boulder. We are stupid. We are selfish. We are animals. What happened to civilization? What happened to common courtesy? What happened to us? Where did our compassion go? Where did humanity go? Where are we headed? Why do I have so many questions that shouldn't even exist? I've always wanted to believe in people and give them a chance. After today, I say fuck them all. I've lost all hope for all of mankind. We're stealing from and killing our fellow man. We're not gonna last very long. We're just doing this to ourselves. Why are we so destructive? I mean, c'mon! WHAT THE HELL IS WRONG WITH US?! I HATE the disease of humans! I say give the world back to the animals. They at least have SOME civility and wouldn't slowly kill the world just for gain and profit. When and how will this all end?

There will be no winner, we've already all lost.

### The Strive 08-15-2005

Did you ever want to be something better than what you are? "Hasn't everybody", right? Shouldn't we see this as a problem? Obviously nobody is happy; nobody likes who they are or where they're at in their life, and yet nobody cares or wants to do anything about it.

Who can do something about it; what can be done?

"You"; "take that first step towards change".

We're always trying to run from change. Spending all of our time, money, and energy to keep things the way they are. This brings me back to my first stipulation that nobody likes who they are. Then why are we struggling so hard against the natural flow of change if we don't like the current situation? Are we afraid that things will get much more worse that we'll want the original design, but are at a point of no return and have to settle back into the "fear of change' routine? Is this what has happened to this world? Have we failed so many times that we'd rather just lie broken, busied, and bleeding on the ground; that we don't want to get up, dust off, and strive forward, again, for something better? Or is it that we're now in the mindset that there is no "better" left to strive towards?

We need a slap in the face and a good swift kick in the butt.

"To fail is human and forgivable; to give up is eternal self damnation"

### Paper Toys 08-17-2005

It shouldn't be this way:

Hating every breath of life. Never being able to explore this life to my fullest extent. Not given a chance to succeed, and when given once, snatched away like a priceless object in the hands of an infant and replaced with the worn-out, broken toy of yesterday. Why is it so hard for someone to try to do better for themselves and their own? What happened to that world of infinite possibilities? Where is my permanent chance at success in life, or at least my chance to just live? Why is money such an issue? Necessities, like water, a place to sleep, and clothing should not be paid for in pain and blood. Why are we killing ourselves and dying just to live and survive? There's something terribly wrong with worshiping and revolving lives around a rectangular, green piece of paper.

### The Boy Who Could Fly 05-19-2006

Contradictions in myself forge forward creating a new sense of self being, positive to counteract the negative, a plan of action, the means to a beginning not an end, blossoms out of the dank and dirt, never to know the touch of darkness again, a soft warm caress, chills down my spine, bumps in new places, pleasure beyond compare, satisfaction and contentment swim together in pure bliss, ripples pool outward to the edge, teasing the cracked dry, taunting it with droplets of unknown joy, the jealous all gone, replaced with a yearning of understanding, combined with the guilt and contemplations is what siphons all moisture and leaves it lifeless.

Alone I am not, I see that now, but is it too late to atone for this mistake? I brandish the whip, I lash myself bloody, but who will tell me that I've had enough? I try to make it right, correct all the wrong, but I never learned that some things stay broken. My thoughts, that's me, it's always been me and the way that I've viewed things. It's time to change, point again to the sky, and hope and dream of the day that I'll fly.

# Inspirational Others

**Transcendence** by Tracy Cune Stansbury

The Earth is ablaze around me,

I do not feel it's warmth.

The screams that echo through the depths evade my ear.

My imagination takes the hand of my soul

and takes it quickly away from reality.

The darkened sky slips out of sight, as it sinks below my feet.

No longer do I breathe it's poison.

The weight of the world's sorrow and pain no longer hold me down.

And gravity looses all purpose and slowly I rise into the heavens,

slipping out of Hell's hands that reach so desperately at my feet.

A calm blue takes over my heart as the red looses all life.

And I close my eyes to the torment and open them to peace.

No longer am I dead.


**Soul Shower** by Misty Re'nee Short

As I lay down in the shower,

Tears stream down,

Long and hard,

Bitter and sour...

I wipe away the steam from the mirror

Things in my mind become clearer...

Dripping with hot wet,

I feel things I haven't felt yet,

Feeling confused and despondent,

I can't seem to comprehend,

Where I'm at is not where I've been,

and what I've looked at is not what I've seen...

I'm sleepy and yet refreshed,

My soul is cleansed and

I'm at my best.

## Crack (Belligerent) by Misty Re'nee Short

The sun is up your bum you crusty whore

There's a monkey on your back, so make the monkey go away

With a hammer from the hardware store

Want to lick the spoon of life and make love to a strobe light

Gonna kiss your pineapples if you let me

Won't you tease me?

Knock knock

Open the damn door

Tick tock

Fix the fucking clock

I'm not Cinderella, but you are one twisted fella

Pumpkin orange dream come true

Brittle bones don't know

Skittles fa la la la la la la la la la

Let's go to the rainbow disco drag queen show!

Woo, woooooooooooo oooa ooo!

Astro bovine, the Queen's soul is fine

Cell phone

GO HOME!

Trapped in an opaque bubble orb

And this I could not absorb

Shamrock tongue & I ate it for fun

Traveling to the desert black sun

I should've taken a plane…

**Still Walking** by Cree

I want to walk in sandals
Like my Jesus did
No house of money changers
My Father did forbid!
No money on the table
The sand beneath my feet
I feel the breeze upon my face
My enemy's defeat.
I see the pictures of you
But we know that they are fake
Father, we live within each other's hearts
And our sandals they can't take.

**Just A Beggar** by Cree

Why do you hurt me when I'm so alone?

To maul me and chew me like a dog with a bone.

As I stand in the streets like a beggar- So cold... So cold...

You sit in your palace so wicked and bold.

You take the child, the flesh of my womb,

and you try to send her deep into the tomb of darkness where you live.

Never being able to forgive.

You leave her crying, sometimes dying.

As we stand up in the streets like beggars- So cold... So cold...

You had a very twisted tree, one to which we clung.

That is the same twisted tree from which we both were hung.

We gave our hearts, we gave our all to fix that twisted tree.

Now you pull our jackets off as we stand in the streets.

Like beggars- So cold... So cold...

But I see the things that you do not see:

The sun on my face, the snow in my shoes,

the voice of an angel, the feel of the blues,

the thoughts of God, and (Ha!) the snow in my shoes.

As I stand up in the streets.

Just a beggar- So cold... So cold...

I hold my head up to the night,

and pray to God with all my might

that all the hatred goes away and we shall see a brighter day.

As we walk in the streets like beggars- So cold... So cold...

Prayers are answered in the strangest ways.

For we will walk the streets one day, paved of gold.

For we took the time to give, the time to pray,

as we walked the streets as beggars- So cold... So cold...

Take our hearts and take our goals,

but you can never take our souls.

For we will walk the streets of gold.

No more pain and no more cold.

For now I walk the streets with the snow in my shoes,

but I take the time to kneel and give thanks.

Just a beggar on the streets - So cold... So cold...

"Hey buddy, got a dime over there? It's snowing pretty hard. Can't get the snow outta my shoes. Too many holes. Keep hoping to get a better pair but, hell, just look at ol' Jake over there with his toes in the wind, just dreaming that it's summertime. He ain't no damned fool! He's warm in his heart, so it keeps his feet warm. Damned if he don't think his street is paved. Well, I'll see ya. Gotta take the baby on down to the mission. Got some food for thought there. Damned snow. Damned shoes."

–Cree (a.k.a. Cindy/Mama)

**Simple** by Deborah Bodine

Copper is nice
Silver is better
Gold is shiny
A diamond is forever
But copper turns black
and silver gets dusty
A diamond can shatter
Even gold can get rusty
A tree is strong
A leaf is pretty
Dew is lovely
Cute is a kitty
But the tree will die
and the leaf falls flat
Dew goes away
A kitty turns into a cat
Hate will diminish
But love will always be
Hate is the lock
But love is the key.

**Parting** by Deborah Bodine

I slowly circled the
clearing in the dark.
Eyes searching the hollows
and shadows for my mark.
Every step a mute,
light touch on the ground.
The giant trees swayed,
letting strong moonlight stream around.

The smell of dirt was strong,
my body low to the ground.
Muscles were ready to spring
when I heard the sound.
My quarry trapped in the open,
danger in the woods, it's prison wall.
The trees above swayed and creaked,
and brilliant stars held me in thrall.

It's heartbeat was quickening,
as if it knew it's fate.
Claws contracted fast,
yet it's panic was too late.
I slowly brought it down
in a blur of fur and blood.
The trees swayed and parted,
the wind came in like a flood.

**Call Me A Liar** by Arielle Duncan

I've done it again, lied to you
Put a knife to your back and pushed it through.
I lied to myself
I said I didn't need help.

I didn't stay with you or hold you close,
I wasn't there when you needed me most.
And now my soul and throat are raw,
And the demon inside me begins to gnaw.

I burst into flame; I'm completely lost,
As I hold your body to me lined with a frost.
How many are gone now because of my fear?
How many more will vanish in the future, so near?

Dropping your body I climb to my feet,
I look to the west and the innocents I'll meet.
Death in my wake; I am consumed by a fire,
I've done it again, call me a liar.

**<u>Grace Full</u>** by Dawn Head

The innocent smile so beautiful

Begs for my time

But it seems as if

There's none to spare

I teach her simplicity

How to pluck the flowers

Taste their sweet nectar

And she tells me

Here's a yellow, Mama

You have it

So I suck it dry

All the yellow inside me

Yet there's none to give away

Almost as if there's no hope

Left for her

Her future so bleak

I look at it and

see my past so awful

Can I change it for her?

So I pluck another yellow

And tell her

You have it

And she smiles so beautiful

And walks away

Pure fluid grace.

**For Brad** by Dawn Head

As the drama unfolds

You find yourself in the center of it all,

cameras flash

That brilliant smile

Yet it is pasted on

And the act begins

Being someone you're not

Afraid of them finding out

Maybe you could learn yourself

The fantasy continues

No holds barred; uninhibited

Thespian splendor: the act

Then the credits roll,

And you find it's really real

Alone in your room

It's who you are

The one who scrawls poetry

On the sidewalk notebook

With love in his heart

But confusion on his face.

**Testosterone** by Dawn Head

Real men don't watch football

Real men watch sunsets

Real men don't spit or cuss

Real men change diapers

Real men don't build hot rods

Real men build relationships

Real men weep

Real men give hugs

Real men giggle

And they always understand
when you have P.M.S.

Or when there's a sale at Wal-Mart!

Which brings up the question:

Are there any real men left?

Yeah…

…they're all gay.

It Always Ends with a Little Something

## **Me** 06-13-2005

Lovelorn, and weary, and lustered, and busted
Given and hoped for, blearily trusted
Taken for granted this boy of emotion
Tossed back, a bad catch from his self-made ocean
Please don't forsake me, my goddess, my passion
Tear down these thresholds forged of cold fashion
Make me immortal and lost in your pages
Lulled soft and tucked deep to sleep there for ages
Lie dormant, sweet nectar, until you're awaken
Enthrall me again, once mentally taken
Stay here, inside me, my inspirational other
Entice me, but spare me, my dark loving lover


My art and fluidity; my essence; the instinct and addiction.

something